South Texas Experience:
Love Letters

Noemi Martínez

South Texas Experience:
Love Letters

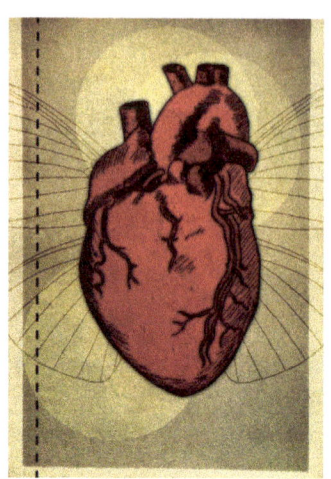

South Texas Experience: Love Letters
Copyright © 2015 by Noemi Martinez

All rights reserved. This book or any portion may not be reproduced or used in any manner whatsoever without the express written permission of the publisher except for the use of brief quotations in a review or scholarly journal.
First Printing: 2015

Hermana Resist Press
http://www.hermanaresistpress.com
Weslaco, TX US

South Texas Experience: Love Letters

for the stars walking under our sky

For Juanita Garza

No seasons
I am looking again
for cold
Make this home
Make this home

And now, I get it. I get it. I get it.
we are anchored here
afraid to get burned like
the white yucca in blossom
the burning grass

I could have grown anywhere
no snow, I drive, drive, drive-
endless streets of the valley

The streets always led me
 where the grass is burned
because rain never reaches us,
I have hated this

In March the orange blossoms
save me

What is that thing called where you know your third great great great great grandmother Maria Luz was born about 1794 on your dad's side and she had a son with Andres in 1816 named Julio. Julio marries Petra, whose parents are Esperidion and Manuela. Petra had a daughter in 1861 in Cerralvo, Nuevo Leon-Marcela. Marcela marries Jacinto. They have a son in 1899, Jose Maria. Jose Maria marries Santiaga. Santiaga has a son in 1944, my dad. Santiaga was born in 1910. Her parents were Cecilio and Jaquina. Jaquina's mother was Simona Alvarado, born in 1863. Her mother's name was Alonsa Gonzalez.

This photo is of Isabel, my mom's Mom, and her dad. It says so on the back. I don't know his name. Lines are tied with histories I do not have access to. What are those missing parts called?

My love letter to you is this, South Texas. There are parts of me that do not belong here. Do not fit here. I cannot recover from a history that I do know/do not know. I am home, yet I am not. I write of my self, my people-Mexican, my home-South Texas, the recovery of our history. Historian as curandera; poet as curandera. But from these borderlands and another. Gloria's wound is half of my tongue, the other half is buried.

South Texas Experience: Love Letters

I could fall in love with you-
Selena

You birthed me South Texas. El Valle-
the magical Rio Grande Valley-
I dream of you when I'm gone.
I hug the roads that bring me back here-
home.
In the white filled streets of Oklahoma,
I longed for the valley.
I visited parks and bodies of water,
sat under the tallest trees I've seen.
They weren't you-
your Sal del Rey,
your isla,
and I missed you.

In cold sterile rooms of Houston,
I waited.

Not a person, no.
You, border lands
You, home, you bloodied me,
swallowed me, made me.

I could lose my heart tonight-
                              Selena

You changed me, I grew in you
I hated you. I needed you. I left.

You-magic valley, made me a witch,
a llorona, a bruja.

I grew out of you.
I grew into you.
I came home.

Home where I can be in Weslaco or
Edinburg or Donna
and summer nights
chicharras sing me to sleep

Home

Decomposed

composed of parts
that I carry with me
not willing to part with them

I have learned
of the wild western frontier
where vigilante mobs roamed at will
where stereotypes of lawlessness
are rewritten into narratives
of people that look like me

I've learned of the
formal procedures of manipulation
finessed to an art form:history

now
what I've always known
 in my bones and traces of cells
control the narrative

History Books in Texas

we write on fraying hems
wait
see what settles

I hear with a wide brush
painting me out
painting us out

In which hopeful souls cross through

Scattered through the dusty grass
Nobody cares about dead immigrants
The terrain is tough and sandy

Water supplies are quickly drained. Bodies overheat rapidly.

Found inside a milk crate.
A milk crate. Human remains.
Reports emerged of bodies buried.

They were driven from McAllen
to just south of the Falfurrias checkpoint,
from where they would have to travel
some 40 miles on foot.

The dusty grass.
Skulls were wedged between coffins.
Small metal markers with the words *Unknown*.

They're invisible when they're alive.
They're invisible when they're dead.

No cemetery

Nobody cares about dead immigrants.

 No map. Human remains. A single grave.
Buried in kitchen trash bags.
In a burlap bag; other remains.
To grieving families:
here is the box labeled *Skeletal Remains*.

Love them like they were
yours, South Texas
Spirits now rest with us
walking hand in hand
or whispering revolution
in the ears of the living

Love them despite
how we discarded their bones
in trash bags
Layered and layered
inside kitchen bags
in makeshift burials
Femur bone touching someone
else's skull or fingers

Love them without names
Hiding under the weight of bodies
Alien to you South Texas

Love them like the stars were lost
one night eyes closing on dreams
of el otro lado
Love them now-South Texas

Redemption

I tried to paint you from memory
your name was erased

-historical trauma

It's so hard to love you texas

with your death and denial
when you choke the stars
before they reach their destination
when you deny your children
born on your dirt
under your sky

it's so hard to love you texas
with your dry dust
trees don't reach the sky
with burnt memories

they call you a prison
we can't get out
The Valley pulls us back
but how can home be a prison
when you hold my secrets in sanctuary
watched my monsters manifest
hold my ghosts in your dirt
how can I leave them
I keep them alive
they keep me alive

my mother,
my longest lover
imperfect lover
forked my border tongue
kept this wound alive
It's so hard to love you Texas

we were candles
burning

I dream of bones with skin and flesh
bring me flowers
I said -no one has brought me flowers
in life or death
as he pins a corsage on my bare chest
a grey blooming one, petals wide

I dream of death and water
and they seep into my poems
Smell of dirt with words like bones

I dream of walls
the dead
bring me ofrendas to write about them

South Texas Experience: Love Letters

found
 inside
a milk crate. Skulls were found in kitchen trash
bags, with as many as many as many as many as
   many as
     many
        as many
as many as
many as many as many as many
as many as many as many as many
as many
       as many as many as many
as
many as many
as
many
     as many
as
  many
 as many
as many
      as many as many as many as
    many as many as
many
      as many as many as many as many
as many as many as
    many as
many as
 piles of
   bodies
burlap
bags, with
    as
many as many as many as many as many
as many
  as many as many
  as many

Home You Learn to Love

Black dragon flies, dozens of them
outside in the yard

crop dusters
we hear every so often at dusk

Tiny frogs appeared after the last hurricane scare,
the size of my thumb.

 Pale green, hide in between the front screen door

this is home home home
this is a season you learn to love

this is home
learn to love
this is home

dry heat
humid heat
rainy heat
tropical heat
this is a season
home you learn to love

Forecast

extremely hot and humid
conditions will lead to
heart constraints
oppressive conditions
continue to surround
the valley, blankets
of heat and hate
110-117 degrees on Friday

Check the children
in uniforms, caged.
It's persistent, I close
my eyes, ears, the door.

It's there
the birds mask
the boy being beaten.
We look in the air,
pray for silence.

Look at the bird
on the fence,
rabbit playing in
the fields,
pretend the worst
does not happen
will not happen

Our backs turn
tune out

it's not happening
it's not happening
it's not happening

prolonged exposure
can lead to
desensitization
remain inside

Río Bravo

Shadows climb the wall
olive sparrows perdónenme
slices of imprint/dna perdónenme
I am of that river

my tongue slipping over pebbles, defined
rivers, eating riverbed during winters
seek refuge entre palabras, walls. Entre
palabras, walls.

jacanas del valle perdónenme
i was of that winter's flight
seeking entrance

half my tongue slipping over pebbles
slices of imprint/dna perdónenme

our bodies in the dirt

Gaze tonight over growing weeds
dying specks of light which appear
sometimes our bodies
with the dirt that fills us
coasting in the lightness

Tumbled and discarded
broken bones
dying specks of light
dying earth -flying- coasting
in the lightness

Roots intertwine with legs
dying specks of light
sometimes our bodies-the dirt
fills the morning

Roots intertwine with legs
In those fleeting moments our bodies
dying specks of light

Weslaco Campus

tufts of grass mounded together
burned by the sun alternate
between gashes of hot asphalt
on expressway 281
if you exit on border ave or international blvd
you've gone to far to meet me

but if you go down border ave
pass the post office
you'll see old trains left
there, rotting rusting, tagged that run
along the back of STC

we walked down there today
sun going down on the fallen sign-
summer classes soon
missing students and empty car lots
cop shows up as
we inspect forgotten buildings

Records for the Dead

Tucked into one pocket of her shorts
A ring on the middle finger of her left hand
She wore a Gold's Gym t-shirt
A boy about age five
four other bags of remains
Other bags of remains
Some of the remains carried notes
A series of numbers
pink Converse sneakers with pink laces
She carried clues, though. She carried clues
She was wearing earrings
some of the remains carried seeds

*One corpse was wrapped in a burlap
bag; other remains were found
inside a milk crate. Skulls were
wedged between coffins*

Texas My Texas

Texas eyes
Look away
blood on dirt
the smell of water and cigarettes
Texas air on our limbs
exposure to eminent danger
eminent domain
we
Do not belong here
to us

Texas my Texas
Our eyes are upon you
native flowers will
sprout in the places
they kill us
Texas, mother of heroes,
comes for our children, still

Texas
we are losing faith
you take our stars
into dust and cells and prisons
Under thin layers of plastic bags and dirt

Inheritances

Cook County Hospital, no pain meds for mom.
Sharing a room with the welfare moms. Lawndale,
Mexican barrio.

Star path towards Cerralvo, South Texas grip not
releasing us. Mom's Motown y tambien Ramon Ayala;
pasteles, tamales y mofongo. Radio Cristiana, born
sinners, la migra, the fields y ramas de mesquite.

De eso y muchas cosas más

There is no inheritance. There are no letters, no
hidden boxes, no family bible, no white
handkerchiefs.

Somos pasajeros

discarded
near the river. you see things like razors.
deodorant. old towels. plastic bags-contents, a
sock, one pair of underwear. a toothbrush.

Noemi Martínez

city
ghosts of yesterday

the canal walk

the canal

and pleade

to acknowledge history

ask about the stars
that die inside
Texas prison walls

For You Again

Keep thinking of those holes
you dig for ten bucks each
deep drenches for ranches
a bandana in your back pocket.
 The sweat falls
into the sweet earth
sees your years
 waits for you

What goes through your head now
living east of the valley
displaced home of ours
twenty sum years
the threads of our roots
spread out thinly
our names mean nothing
deep in earth,
mean nothing here

You travel back
to that place,
a room 10x10
you never say
         much
these lives
overlap
your story
waits

Something
has
died
inside
these
walls.

How much longer? The man shrugged.

Her dad holding hands with a smile

frontage road leads further south escaping

I have that look in a fire

the image of horror and the grave all is not lost

my recollection a plunge into nothingness

her dad holding hands with a fire

I was a fire

Notes:

-Anzaldua, Gloria. *Borderlands / La Frontera: The New Mestiza.* Fourth Edition edition. San Francisco: Aunt Lute Books, 2012.
-Carrigan, William D. *The Making of a Lynching Culture: Violence and Vigilantism in Central Texas, 1836-1916.* University of Illinois Press, 2004.
-Carrigan, William D., and Clive Webb. *Forgotten Dead: Mob Violence against Mexicans in the United States, 1848-1928.* Oxford University Press, 2013.
-Eromosele, Diana Ozemebhoya. "Texas Makes Changes to History Textbooks: No Mention of KKK or Jim Crow, and the Civil War Was Fought Over States' Rights, Not Slavery." *The Root*, July 8, 2015. http://www.theroot.com/
-"Migrant Mass Graves in South Texas May Violate Law." *The Texas Observer*. http://www.texasobserver.org/
-Morales, Aurora Levins. *The Historian as Curandera.* Julian Samora Research Institute, Michigan State University, 1998.
"Rising Immigrant Deaths Put Burden on Texas County." *CNS News.* http://www.cnsnews.com
-*The Real Death Valley: The Untold Story of Mass Graves and Migrant Deaths in South Texas.* https://vimeo.com/102926113.
"in which hopeful souls cross through"

I Could Fall in Love-Selena from the album "Forever Selena." Written by Kieth Thomas.

Photos:
La Sal Del Rey, Edinburg, Texas-cover, xii, ii, 1,10,11, 16, 22-23, 24, Weslaco, Texas-31, 34, 35, back cover.

Some of these poems have appeared in: *Yellow Chair Review, Lines from Acedia to Apatheia*

Noemi Martinez is a writer, poet-curandera and media myth maker with Mexican and Caribbean roots living in the militarized borderland of deep South Texas, birthplace of Gloria Anzaldúa. She is a radical single mami with punk tendencies. A long time zinester, she started her first zine, *Making of a Chicana* in 2000 and *Hermana, Resist* in 2001. She has also written the zines *Aged Noise, Homespun* and *Sofrito Pa' Ti*. She edited the *Voces* collection, *MAIZ* collection and was co-editor of the anthology *For Colored Girls*. She has been a part of larger collaborative networks to share independent alt.media as activism. She founded and directed two community groups, CAFE Revolucion and Voices Against Violence. She is a cofounder of the Gloria Anzaldúa Legacy Project.

Some of her poems can be found in *¡Ban This! The BSP Anthology of Xican@ Literature* and essays in the following collections: *Don't Leave Your Friends Behind: Concrete Ways to Support Families in Social Justice Movements, Communities, Labor Pains and Birth Stories: Essays on Pregnancy, Childbirth and Becoming a Parent* and *Just Like a Girl: A Manifesta!* Recently her poems and photos have been published in *Make/Shift, Hip Mama, Xicana Chronicles, Pentimento, The Perch, Star 82 Review, Yellow Chair Review, TAYO Literary Magazine* and *Revolutionary Motherhood: Love on the Frontlines*. She has an undergraduate degree from the University of Texas-El Paso and a Master's degree in writing and history.

Photos by Jonathan River Hernandez-Martinez, a teen aspiring photographer from South Texas.

www.ingramcontent.com/pod-product-compliance
Lightning Source LLC
Chambersburg PA
CBHW061248230426
43663CB00021B/2944